Susan Cain's

Quiet

The Power of Introverts in a World That Can't Stop Talking

Summary by Ant Hive Media

Please Note

This is a Summary & Analysis of the original book, available here: http://amzn.to/1RTqca9. Or, visit http://amzn.to/1WpoTBi for easy listening.

You can get two Audio Books of your choice FREE with Audible now. Simply start your digital membership here: http://amzn.to/1WpoTBi and choose the books you want.

Copyright © 2016 by Ant Hive Media.

Limit of Liability/Disclaimer of Warranty:

Table of Contents

A GIFT FOR YOU

As a way of saying thank you we want to
offer you a pack of (5) e-book summaries **FREE!**

Available Here:
www.anthivemedia.com/freesummaries

OVERVIEW

In this review of the book, "Quiet: The Power of Introverts in a World That Can't Stop Talking" by author Susan Cain, we go through a thoroughly detailed synopsis of the main concepts explored by the book and follow this up with a thoughtful analysis. This book takes a look at introversion at a personal, national, institutional and social level. The writer has drawn on her own experience and the experience of others and backed up the concepts with sound scientific research – drawing from fields as diverse as genetic research and psychology.

There are four main sections in the book. In the first section, the idea of the current trend toward the "Extrovert Ideal" that permeates our culture today is discussed. In the second section, the author has a look at the nature-nurture argument as it pertains to the level of introversion or extroversion. It also explores how easy it is to alter these behaviors in terms of this range. The third part looks at the current trends nationally, in particular zoning in on Asian cultures and how they compare to Western ones. In the last section, practical solutions for being successful in spite of introversion are tackled – in social, business and school settings.

The author got her Bachelor's in English through Princeton and a law degree through Harvard School of Law. She practiced as an attorney and also a consultant in negotiations. Her work in the field of introversion has been published in Time Magazine, Psychology Today,

OMagazine and the New York Times. The organizers of TED2012 also invited her to speak.

SUMMARY

INTRODUCTION: THE NORTH AND SOUTH OF TEMPERAMENT

This opening chapter sets the tone for the rest of the work and explains why the topic is so important. We begin by looking at the traits of two well-known individuals, Martin Luther King Jr. and Rosa Parks, and how they were able to effect great change: Parks in the calm manner in which she faced confrontation and King in the way that he communicated his message to so many people. Though very different, they were both responsible for sweeping changes in the American psyche.

According to Cain, the career path we chose, who we make friends with, how many risks we are willing to take and even the synaptic pathways in our brains are influenced by where we rate on the temperament spectrum. Cain highlights that despite out current trend to favor those who are more extroverted, but as much as half of the populace can be classified as introverts. She has coined the term "Extrovert Ideal" to explore this cultural bias towards the extroverted. It is this system of values that can negatively impact introverts and lead to the actual strength of the introvert going unnoticed at work and in society in general.

Cain has, through her practice, assisted introverts to focus on their own particular strengths in all aspects of their lives. Her own experience as an introvert gave her a unique understanding of learning to master these techniques and learning to accept her own personal strengths as well.

She does take some time out to have a look at the basic definitions of extroversion and introversion, but also reminds us that there is no set definition in place and that it is not as simple as classifying people as extrovert or introvert. She does stress that the context is just as important as the behavior in determining a person's basic leanings one way or another. She offers a quick quiz to allow you to see where you might be on the spectrum. The overall aim of the book is not to classify, however, but rather to aid introverts and the people closest to them.

PART ONE: THE EXTROVERT IDEA

CHAPTER 1
HOW THE EXTROVERT IDEAL CAME INTO BEING

The first chapter looks at how society first started to develop the bias toward extroversion, beginning in the earlier parts of the 20th century. According to Warren Susman, an historian, the so-called Character Culture emphasized the importance of being introspective, moral, serious and self-disciplined. The alternative Personality On the other hand, Culture, which was swiftly adopted with increased urbanization, emphasized the importance of the perception of others and emphasized charisma as the driving force behind success.

Cain theorizes that it was the increase in urbanization and the subsequent necessity to deal with strangers on a more regular basis that facilitated this shift.

Cain examines the shift from several different angles. She starts with the movement toward self-help – a longtime favorite among American readers. If you look at publications before the early part of the 20th century, you will see that reflection, high morals and modesty are praised. Take a look at books from the 1920's onward and you will notice a determined shift in the way the books were marketed. Prior to this, it was the information contained in the book that was the main selling point. After this, the emphasis shifted toward success through altering the perception of others – advertising moved more toward the books providing a "cure" for a reader's social defect.

The field of psychology also started to reflect these changing attitudes. Gordon Allport devised a test to determine where people fell when it came to social dominance. Jung's efforts made a significant contribution to the new ideal as well. It may however be that Alfred Adler had the most influence when it came to the adoption of this new ideal with his theory of the "inferiority complex." This idea was readily adopted by the press and several warnings about this complex and ways to get over it were published.

The experts at the time started to look out for shy children and began issuing dire warnings of what could happen if this issue was not addressed. As a result, the idea of introversion was a problem that needed to be corrected became embedded at an institutional level. Parents quickly fell in line with this idea, thinking they were doing what was best for the child and "fitting in" became the new ideal. Children began to attend school at younger ages to encourage extra socialization. This system was more entrenched as the children moved up the ladder at school. Being socially adept became a criterion for access to higher education with the justification that well-rounded students would fit in better in the workplace later in life. This carried forward into the business world as well with better opportunities being afforded to those with better social skills. More and more, those who were seen as introverts began to be regarded as "broken."

Cain does point out that this is not the first instance of such social biases. The difference this time is that there is such an emphasis at this stage that it has invaded every aspect of life. If you were to take a quick look at teenagers today, you would see that a lot of emphasis is placed on their status and how they are viewed by their peers, and how this shapes the adolescent experience. To make things worse, psychology tends to view introversion as a disorder – estimating one in five Americans suffer social anxiety. According to psychological classifications, even the fear of speaking in public can be classified as a disorder. The author closes off the chapter by asking us to think about what has been lost in the move from the emphasis on character to that of personality.

CHAPTER 2
WORSHIPPING AT THE ALTAR OF PERSONALITY

This chapter is centered on the modern trend toward linking extroversion with good leadership skills. Cain draws on examples from the Harvard Business School and personalities, such as Tony Robbins and Rick Warren, to further illustrate this link. She goes on to relate some of her own personal experiences, and those of others in a similar situation, and how they were affected by this standard.

Her overall research, combined with the anecdotal data she has collected, paints a very different picture of extroversion as the ideal model of a leader – not only is it too narrowly defined but in some cases it can also work against people.

Cain starts this chapter with a rundown of a typical motivational seminar she attended that was run by Tony Robbins. Tony Robbins could arguably be called the poster child for the extrovert ideal and it works for him. In his seminars, he promotes the extrovert ideal as the solution for succeeding in life. And the atmosphere at the event seemed to bear out the wisdom of this advice, with dancing and chanting and a lot of interaction with fellow participants. According to Robbins, personal power and the ability to sell ourselves are linked together.

According to Cain, however, this suggests that meeting people and interacting with them is merely a game in which you want to win by getting them to like you, and you are aiming to be the dominant and superior party. The downside of this theory is that you spend more time pretending to be a good person and less time working on becoming one. People who are shy or reserved end up being perceived as being less worthy.

It is not just motivational speakers that adhere to this theory, Harvard Business School has also joined the fray in idealizing extroversion and sets out to cultivate this quality in a number of ways. It is expected that students engage with one another in several different settings outside of the classroom – whether this means as part of a study group or having drinks after school. Those students who prefer not to "socialize" are viewed with suspicion. Cain interviewed an introverted student and found that the constant pressure to be sociable made the time spent at school exhausting and that he felt more isolated. He knew that he had to come across as an extrovert but found that it severely drained his reserves to do so. He had to focus more effort on making conversation and in interacting. These were things that he did not gravitate toward naturally.

The curriculum at the business school pushes the extrovert ideal. Students are graded on how well they worked within a group and how willing they were to participate in class discussions. There is a bias toward group exercises to build team work. Most often, these groups are dominated by one or two students who direct the others. Not really the definition of team work, but this propensity to make decisions quickly and assertively is prized as the sign of a leader.

Cain goes on to argue that we may be incorrect in this assumption from the outset. She noted that there tends to be a bias against those who are quieter in in nature and they are perceived to be not as competent. They tend to be judged on this more than on their good ideas.

Adam Grant, from Wharton, has been doing some interesting research into the relationship between leadership skills and extroversion. His studies show that the correlation between an increase in leadership ability and extroversion are tentative, at best, and are more likely a result of our perception that extroverts make better leaders.

Grant also checked to see whether or not the context would make any difference when it came to leadership styles. He discovered that an introverted leader is the best bet to get high levels of productivity from a team of extraverts and that the reverse was also true. What this means is that the context must also be considered when determining leadership that works – there is no one right answer.

Cain then comes back to Rosa Parks and a more detailed look at what qualities made her so vital to the civil rights movement. She found that it was Park's unassuming and quiet nature that helped build her credibility as the focus of the movement. She built a reputation for being a background player rather than a glory seeker and so helped many more people. Her introverted nature prevented her from being branded a fire brand and made her more credible.

In Malcom Gladwell's book, "The Tipping Point," he looks at what he calls "connectors." These are persons who have made an extraordinary impact in the effort to bring people together. One such connector, Craig Newmark, the brains behind Craigslist, is known as an introvert – more interested in a game of chess or studying physics than in engaging in conversation.

Cain beefs up this list with the addition of Pete Cashmore and Guy Kawasaki, both of whom have made no bones about being introverts and both of whom have had a massive impact on social media and the way that we communicate. These three examples, according to the Harvard Business School, should never have succeeded.

The last bit of this second chapter ends with a note about the Saddleback Church. This is a huge facility that hosts on average 22 000 people during weekly worship. Much in the same way as at Harvard Business School, the extrovert ideal is also held up as the way to go.

Cain visited the campus and spoke to Adam, a pastor who has identified himself as an introvert. Adam raised the issue that modern day evangelism seems to be actively seeking people out and preaching to them. For an introvert, this is difficult and Adam's own struggle had made him wonder if his personality was at odds with what God wanted. He was almost at a stage where he felt as though his nature was causing him to fail spiritually. He felt alone until he started to notice that there were others around him feeling the same pressure. Those who were also battling to find their own niche in a world where leaders were increasingly more charismatic and loud. Adam turned to blogging as a way to deal with these pressures and wrote a book, highlighting the value of quiet contemplation and time away from others as a way to further one's spiritual growth.

CHAPTER 3
NEW GROUPTHINK COMPARED TO SOLO WORK

This chapter deals with what Cain describes as "New Groupthink." This is a means of organizing workplaces, institutions and schools with the assumption that better innovation and creativity result from working in a group. She starts out with a strong argument against this assumption, drawing on an example gleaned from Steve Wosniak's biography. In his biography, Steve regularly states that his most creative ideas and breakthroughs occurred during times when he was alone. While it is important to have a community with which to bounce ideas off, there is no substitute for quite, alone time that allows you to more easily order your thoughts without distractions.

Cain also highlights the fact that research has shown that among those who are creative, introversion is more the rule than the exception. In most cases, creative people prefer to be left alone so that they are able to concentrate more fully. Introverted creatives also tend to prefer to mull over problems in a way that makes sense to them – not in some universally accepted "right" way.

The cold fact is that the modern world seems to overlook these aspects of the creative personality. According to Cain, New Groupthink is a style where teamwork is seen as the most important priority. Malcom Gladwell's "Organizing Genius" actually states that "two heads are better than one". This philosophy has been embraced wholeheartedly by the corporate world, as seen in a survey conducted with people in high-level or senior-management roles. Around 91% of the participants stated that teamwork was vital when it came to overall business success. Team building can come in a number of different forms – team-building exercises, cloud technology, open-plan offices, etc.

Groupthink is also being adopted in a number of standard teaching practices. You no longer walk into a room with desks all facing the front but rather you enter a room that makes use of pod seating. Instead of learning by repetition from the teacher, each group is given a project to work on together, even when it comes to subjects like creative writing and math that do not seem well suited to it. Cain has found that this method of teaching is being quickly adopted, especially with the younger teachers. In order to justify these teaching methods, the idea is that they are better preparing the children for what the corporate world expects. Another justification is that they are training future leaders. In Cain's view, both of these justifications are suspect – "teamwork" is not the be all and end all for all kids and not all kids want to train as leaders.

According to Cain, there isn't really one central location that can be attributed to the initial rise of Groupthink. That said, the internet has been instrumental in helping it spread – making it a lot easier for collaborations to exist. However, it should be noted that collaboration online is a very different prospect from real world interactions and it is the real world interactions that the introverts will struggle with.

Anders Ericsson is a psychologist who has zoned in on the qualities of people who have excelled in their fields. He has looked through a varied range of disciplines considered highly competitive, such as tennis, football, etc. It was he that coined the term "Deliberate Practice" to describe the way that highly motivated people hone their skills through concentration and practice. He found that the best time to undertake this practice is when one is alone – cutting out external distractions and allowing each individual to determine their own level of progress. He brings in examples for Steve Wosniak's biography to show how his own progression was driven by deliberate practice, primarily on his own.

Timothy Lister and Tom DeMarco, in a separate study, found that there was a significant gap between the performance of programmers working in relative solitude and privacy and those that did not. The former group produced higher quality of work despite, in some cases, having less experience.

Other studies conducted in the open=office policy, so popular at the moment, shows that it is not the best model at all – employees are less productive, more likely to be unhealthy and more likely to leave.

In addition, compelling research has been presented that actually shows that brainstorming in a group setting can be ineffective. It is better for individuals to work separately on the ideas they want to present and then pool their ideas. It is thought that even though brainstorming is meant to help quell social anxiety, this really only works on paper –

most of us are still worried that our ideas, and ourselves, will be judged harshly; and that group dynamics will play a big role. This all combines to make a more creative solution less likely.

To make matters worse, studies conducted by Gregory Berns at Emory University show that peer pressure can influence the way we look at the problem – we may be more inclined to think like the dominant group members rather than following our own instincts.

There is a place for real world collaboration and that is not in dispute. However, we do need to apply ourselves when it comes to seeking out the best solution – the adage "too many cooks can spoil the broth" should be considered. A combination of both work in isolation and work as part of a team may be a better way to achieve results, rather than defaulting to a groupthink situation.

Research has shown, for example, that groups where there are similar amounts of extroverts and introverts tend to be more successful. According to Cain, by allowing people a choice when it comes to socializing or not, you give them the best opportunity to shine according to their own strengths. Cain goes on to cite Microsoft and Pixar as examples of companies where this strategy has been successfully applied.

PART TWO: YOUR BIOLOGY, YOUR SELF?

CHAPTER 4
IS TEMPERAMENT DESTINY?

This chapter is an analysis of the nature versus nurture debate when it comes to our own personalities. She starts with a review of research conducted by Jerome Kagan, well-respected in the field of developmental psychology and based at Harvard. A sample population of 500 infants, each 4 months old, was exposed to new experiences ranging from swabs soaked in alcohol to popping balloons. Kagan assumed that the greater the reaction of the infant, the higher the probability that they would become extroverts when growing up. The children were monitored as they grew and it was found the hypothesis to be correct. Kagan theorized that the same area of the brain, the amygdala, controls the heightened sensitivity to external stimuli in babies and higher levels of vigilance when it came to making new acquaintances. Cain agrees that there is a strong correlation but does warn that human behavior is a lot more complex and is seldom attributable to a single cause.

Heightened sensitivity can be linked to increasing levels of alertness and greater focus on stimuli, in terms of Kagan's findings. Those children with heightened sensitivities when tested in their first school year were found to better consider alternatives when it came to matching games and tended toward greater accuracy. These children also appear to feel at a deeper level and are able to pick up on nonverbal cues. What Kagan has found is that some of the factors of introversion can be based on biology. Different studies have also helped further this theory. Studies centered on twins show that there is a correlation when it comes to genetics and introversion – the data seem to indicate that there is a 40%-50% hereditary factor. That said, there is also a good chance that environmental influences play a role.

Cain asked Kagan about his views on the nature versus nurture debate as it relates to a person's temperament. Kagan admitted that while his early career placed him firmly in the nurture side of the equation, his subsequent research has shown him that it is an interaction of both biological and environmental factors that makes the determination in the end. It is possible that the amygdala is only one part of the equation in determining the level of reactivity in a person. He stated that even though we may have found a single part of the equation, the whole is a lot more complex than we initially thought.

The child's developmental environment can play a vital role when it comes to being successful. Children with low levels of reactivity, for example, are more likely to engage in risky behavior and in poorer areas where these risks abound, delinquency is often expected. Jay Belsky, a psychologist from the University of London, and others like him have hypothesized that it is the more sensitive children who are affected the most by their environment. There is a point of view – "the orchid hypothesis" that assumes that adverse experiences during childhood have the greatest impact on children with higher levels of reactivity. Conversely, they reap greater benefits if they are exposed to a more nurturing environment.

The author also draws attention to the fact that this phenomenon has been replicated in studies related to rhesus monkeys. The research with the monkeys zoned in on the SERT gene, the gene that regulates the processing of serotonin. It was found that one variation of the gene, that with a shortened allele, has been linked to increased rates of responsiveness in monkeys and humans. In the monkeys with this variation, stressful situations and environments are prone to have more adverse side effects. According to Stephen Suomi, the researcher, some of that reason can be attributed to how the more responsive monkeys observe more of the social dynamics of the group. In the same manner, teenage girls who have this gene variation are one fifth more inclined to react to stressors with depression. These teenage girls are one fourth less likely to react with depression when the environment is more supportive.

CHAPTER 5
BEYOND TEMPERAMENT

Chapter 5 looks at our capacity to change despite our genetic predisposition. She begins by covering work by Carl Schwartz from the Massachusetts General Hospital in the field of neural imaging. He has focused on neural imaging of the amygdala, in particular, of those same children that took part in Kagan's study, as they moved into adulthood. The initial project focused on producing neural images of the reaction when pictures of strangers were viewed. It was found that there was a correlation between being highly responsive and having more activity in the amygdala region. According to Schwartz, this shows that although we can alter our personality, there are some biologically imposed limits at play as well.

Your amygdala is the most primal part of the brain – this is where instinctive behavior is rooted. As humans though, we also have a neocortex to aid us with more advanced cognitive work. It is here where we make decisions or think about abstract concepts – things that do not require an instinctual response. One of its functions is to assess whether or not we are in real danger or if the fear is unwarranted. People who, for instance, where mapped while performing self-talk exercises designed to be reassuring showed an increase in activity in the neocortex and a similar decrease in activity in the amygdala. It was also shown that should the neocortex be preoccupied, as is the case in a stressful situation, its calming action on the amygdala is less effective.

Cain guessed that this symbiotic relationship between the two areas in the brain allows introverts to learn how to act well in a social setting but that, despite these learned coping behaviors, the stress of being in a social situation can trigger a fear response in the amygdala. On the other side of the coin, the extrovert can take a page from the book of the introvert and benefit from periods of calm and reflection.

Cain draws on many studies of performance to make the point that extroverts and introverts both have differing needs in terms of stimulation to be able to perform optimally. By being self-aware, we can also learn to cultivate these ideal levels of stimulation in our lives to achieve optimal performance. As an example, Cain relates Ester's story – Ester is an introvert who is required to make presentations from time to time. She works with extroverts who find that this is no problem for them and who can make presentations off the cuff. For Ester, on the other hand, the whole experience is made bearable by being given enough time to prepare properly. Because Ester is aware of these limitations, she can request sufficient time to prepare for her presentation and thus reduced her anxiety levels.

In the last portion of the chapter, Cain describes the benefits that she derived from taking part in a support group for public speaking. She was subjected to a desensitization exercise and therapy designed to help her overcome her fear of speaking in public. According to Cain, these techniques were especially useful for her.

CHAPTER 6
FRANKLIN WAS A POLITICIAN, BUT ELEANOR SPOKE OUT OF CONSCIENCE

The theme explored in this section is the positive aspects of being introverted. At the beginning of the chapter, we have a look at Franklin and Eleanor Roosevelt. She was known as a shy, reflexive and serious individual whereas he was known to be bold and outgoing and highly social. This striking difference between the two did lead to friction at times. He craved social interaction and she tried to avoid it, resulting in Franklin having an affair with his wife's secretary. This effectively put an end to any romance in the marriage but they stayed together and the relationship evolved.

Cain looks here to Elaine Aron and her research. Aron has contributed to some of the scientific research alluded to in the book and even challenged it. Aron dislikes Kagan's use of the term "highly reactive" as she feels that it has negative connotations and instead refers to these people as "sensitives".

Aron also worked on extending some of the corresponding associations inherent to the classification of people in this manner. This included finding correlations between sensitives and deeper levels of empathy and a more highly developed sense of moral reasoning. Aron based her research on both clinical work and interviews and this has led to a more complex and broadly defined personality profile.

Studies now have proved that for a long time there is a correlation between sensitivity and a more well-developed sense of conscience. Grazyna Kochanska, an expert in developmental psychology, conducted an experiment to see how children would react if given a toy that was engineered to break. It was found that the introverted children expressed more anxiety or guilt at having broken the toy. As the children grow older, they are more likely to follow the rules even when they know they are not being watched and have much higher levels of empathy. Psychologists have found that people who see another person blushing after committing a misdeed perceive that person as more trustworthy because they are showing outward signs that they realize that they have done something wrong. Basically by displaying embarrassment, the person is indicating that they care about the other party's feelings and thus they are committed to this relationship.

Cain follows this up with the speculation as to possible advantages biologically when it comes to survival that sensitives can have over "normals". She starts off by going through Aron's work and highlighting where Aron believes that sensitives benefit because they tend to consider their options more carefully and tend toward an aversion to risk. Cain then continues that there are at minimum 100 different animal species that exhibit the same sort of behavioral characteristics along the spectrum and that this is an indication that this range of behavior could have some sort of advantage in terms of evolution.

Typically, about a fifth of any sample population will show signs of being introverted. An explanation of this can be found in the evolutionary "trade-off" theory, a theory that has been buoyed up by numerous studies across various species that suggests that diverse strategies increase the odds of survival in changing conditions. Thus, the more diversity there is, the better the chances for survival over time.

Cain also argues that, when considered in the light of Aron's work, it can be said that sensitivity helps to aid survival of the species far beyond the fact that sensitives are less likely to take risks. Sensitives also have a better understanding of the environment and are more observant and can spot potential danger and warn the others as well. In human terms, we can benefit in several different ways. Cain uses the work of Al Gore as an example of the ways in which sensitives have alerted us to environmental dangers.

CHAPTER 7
WHY DID WALL STREET CRASH AND WARREN BUFFETT PROSPER?

This is a bit of a controversial chapter and in it Cain examines the role of reward sensitivity in where we fit in in terms of temperament and how this affects one area of our economy – investments. She starts with an explanation of the idea of "reward sensitivity" and provides scientific proof of it. Those considered reward sensitive are extremely motivated when it comes to potential rewards. Those at the extreme side of the scale could be sensitive to the point that they do not take the potential risks into account.

Janice Dorn, a specialist psychologist works with those who make a living in finance. She identified a correlation between higher levels of reward sensitivity and higher levels of extroversion. According to Dorn, the structure of the brain plays a big role here as well. The amygdala forms part of the limbic system – the pleasure center in the brain and, in some people, particularly those with higher levels of reward sensitivity, this system is more active when rewards are being contemplated. Research seems to back Dorn's theory up as well.

Cain takes things one step further and assumes that this may be one of the leading causes of extrovert behavior. Those who exhibit extrovert behaviors have a higher chance of experiencing mood altering highs when considering potential rewards, and this can make them less likely to be able to see the downside. Neural imaging seems to back this up – the pleasure centers in the brain tend to show greater levels of activity for this type of person when rewards are put on the table.

And more and more studies are beginning to show a distinct difference in the way that such people process dopamine. Extroverts tend to react more strongly to catalysts of dopamine, such as amphetamines, and have more active pathways for processing dopamine.

Cain then moves focus to the idea of investing and presents a number of expert opinions on the way that the extrovert ideal could operate in the current financial sector, especially in relation to the reward sensitive theory. Studies conducted by the Kellogg School of Management have shown a link between the gene that regulates dopamine and the willingness to take risks financially. It is ironic but these risk takers seem to have less success over the long term when it comes to investing when compared to introverts. Cain thought that this is as a result of not being able to consider the risks as rationally in the face of potential rewards. Cain goes on to state that the financial chaos of 2008 could be directly attributed to the propensity to take ill-considered risks.

This statement is countered by Boykin Curry, who was one of the managing directors of a financial investing firm throughout the crises. He says that the overall culture at the time was geared toward taking more risks when investing and that extroverts were the preferred investment managers at the lead up to the crises. The short term picture was a rosy one – with people making more use of leverage and taking higher risks and reaping higher rewards. In the lead-up to the crash, such investors had made excellent returns and so garnered better reputations and more power. At the time, those who were the most reward sensitive were the natural choices for leadership positions across the sector, and those who practiced a more cautious approach were actively left out when it came to promotions.

A professor at Rice University and onetime Enron employee, Vincent Kaminski also described something similar in the lead up to the failure of Enron. In both cases, warnings issued by more conservative investors and experts fell on deaf ears.

Cain does not agree with the general impression that introverts make better investments because they are less risk averse and offers evidence to back her opinion. She cites a study conducted by the University of Wisconsin's Joseph Newman where he compared how extroverts reacted when it came to the assessment of long-term risk. He set up a system of flashing numbers and assigned either positive or negative point values to these numbers when the appropriate button was pushed. It was found that introverts were more likely to be more cautious than extroverts after having picked a wrong number and were less likely to choose that number again by accident. According to Newman, the risk takers take less time when it comes to the processing of negative feedback and this hurts their abilities when it comes to accurately assessing risk.

According to Cain, there are two basic solutions when it comes to determining which of the temperaments will perform best when it comes to financial investment. She starts off by arguing that a successful investor will have aspects of both – allowing them to draw on the advantages of each type. She then also suggests that getting to know what your own temperament is when it comes to risk taking is a good way to optimize your own performance.

Lastly in this chapter, Cain looks at investors who not only rode out the 2008 crises but did so in style. Baupost Group's Seth Klarman was one of the ones discussed because he adopted a more cautious approach during the crises and so doubled the company's assets. Michael Burry, a manager of a hedge fund who, despite being an introvert, was highly critical of the investment stance that led up to the crash. Warren Buffet took a lot of flak from the more extroverted investors when he foresaw the demise of the dot com – he was proved tight within the year. Cain encourages her readers to adopt a more cautious approach when it comes to making investment decisions.

PART THREE: DO ALL CULTURES HAVE AN EXTROVERT IDEAL?

CHAPTER 8
SOFT POWER

Here Cain deals with the idea of the extrovert ideal being a Western cultural phenomenon and compares it to the "soft power" approach more typical in the East. This "soft power" style of leadership is not about being bold and brash. The main body of the chapter revolves around interviews with students who are either Asian born or Asian American. She does, however, also bring in some data in support of her hypothesis.

She first draws on examples from the Cupertino school system where, in a twist, white families have been moving out of the community in a bid to spare their kids the highly competitive school environment and because they fear that their kids are unable to compete with the large number of highly driven Asian kids. In fact, academics in this environment is so important that your typical sports jocks that tend to feature so highly elsewhere barely feature here at all. A lot of students do realize that the culture at university will be a lot different and more socially based. Cain argues that the very unique character of Cupertino can be attributed to Asian cultural norms where study is valued and deference is shown to authority figures.

Cain goes on to say that the education style of Asia tends toward more focus on the authority of the teacher. Student participation is only encouraged when it enhances the discussion and when the ideas are properly formulated. On the other hand, your typical American education tends to encourage participation in general, even when it is unfocused or not particularly useful. In such circumstances, an Asian student may be mistaken as being an unwilling participant or as not understanding the material when, in fact, they are not participating out of deference to the teacher.

Cain lists research conducted by Robert McCrae and many others that shows the difference culturally between Eastern and Western cultures, painting a picture of Asian cultures being more inclined to be more introverted. This difference can cause a real problem for Asians trying to make their way in U.S. companies. The point that she is raising here is not that one style is better than the other, but simply that the extrovert ideal currently embraced is not the only one and is not necessarily a natural evolution either. Seen from this angle, we understand that "ideal" leadership depends on the context and historical culture.

During the interviews conducted with the Asian professionals, Cain did note that they were aware that there was a gap in their comfort with the extrovert behavior and the expectation that this was what is expected to succeed in America. A professor of communication, Preston Ni, does workshops to help foreign professionals develop successful techniques for communication in American society. Cain interviewed him after having attending a workshop and asked what his opinion was of the extrovert ideal. Ni assumed that it was possible to adapt and fit in but that it should also be known that other leadership styles, such as soft power ones, also have benefits.

Kindness, respect for the rights of your fellow man, persistence and quiet conviction are aspects of soft power. Buda, Gandhi and Mother Theresa are shining examples of how powerful soft power really is.

PART FOUR: HOW TO LOVE, HOW TO WORK

CHAPTER 9
WHEN SHOULD YOU ACT MORE EXTROVERTED THAN YOU REALLY ARE?

This chapter looks at the ethics behind and strategies that allow you to adopt extroverted behavior. Before she really gets stuck into the main premise though, she explores the controversy evident in literature of a psychotically nature as it pertains to how valid it is to define and ascribe certain stable traits of personality. This is referred to as the "person-situation£ controversy. At the person end, the spectrum implies that everyone has a basic personality and traits evident throughout life. At the other end of the scale, it is implied that personality can change in accordance with experiences.

Now retired, Brian Little, a Professor of Psychology at Harvard, was the one that originally came up with the ideas that Cain discusses in this chapter. His main contribution to our current understanding of psychology is known as the "Free Trait Theory" in which he assumed that while a balance of cultural and biological predispositions helps us form a basic core of traits that are reasonably stable, we are able to alter them to allow us to achieve more success. If the goal we are striving for is of particular importance, it is relatively simple to make the appropriate adjustments in personality.

People are able to build on their skills when they adopt these so-called free traits. Some people, those that are better at "self-monitoring" (a skill that can be honed) are also better when it comes to copying the behaviors of different personalities when required. Cain offers questionnaires to help you identify your own skills in self-monitoring. That said, Cain does caution against taking it too far. If you attempt to alter your basic personality traits in order to accomplish something that you are not invested in, you are more likely to cause yourself stress and could even burn out.

Cain does give some guidance as to how you can identify your projects in keeping with your own core personality. Start off by reanalyzing the dreams you had as a child, looking this time not at the job but the qualities that drew you to it – what excited you about it. Maybe you wanted to be a fireman, for example. Looking back, that might indicate that you want a job that involves helping people, some adventure and some risk. Perhaps being a fireman is not an option any longer but can you perhaps think of something else that might be a good fit in terms of those qualities? Secondly, you can look at those who have the jobs that you would love to do and analyze the characteristic qualities of these jobs.

Cain goes on to suggest that you take the time to create a sanctuary for yourself for those times when you have had to step out of you comfort zone. In this space, the real you can come into play. For an introvert, this could be a calm space where they can be alone. For an extrovert, it might be a visit to a club or some other type of social engagement. These little mini-breaks let you recharge so you are better able to face the stresses of the day and can more easily move out of your comfort zone more.

CHAPTER 10
THE COMMUNICATION GAP

Romantic and fulfilling partnerships are possible even between partners on opposite sides of the introversions/extroversion spectrum. Cain does, however, stress that having a successful relationship under these circumstances is contingent on each party understanding the other's needs and being sensitive of them. Cain provides examples from research and takes an in depth look at some clinical instances.

According to research, labelling introverts as being antisocial is incorrect. The truth is that a lot of introverts are very social but prefer a more intimate gathering to a large crowd. It is true that extroverts typically have a greater number of friends but this is often a case of quantity over quality. Susanne Wilpers and Jens Aspendorf, in the psychology department of Humboldt University, have tracked the "big five" of psychology – agreeableness, willingness to experience new things, introvert/extrovert, conscientiousness and mental stability in a sample of 132 university students in conjunction with their relationship patterns.

Those who had the smallest amount of conflict at a relationship level scored high in terms of agreeableness and displayed no real signs of differences when it came to the introvert/extrovert scale. Cain also provides research results that indicate that it would seem that extroverts prefer relationships that are more competitive while extroverts prefer ones that are more cooperative. In a different study it was found that patients classified as introverts reacted better when robots used soothing and caring tones while patients classified as extroverts reacted better when forceful or commanding tones were used.

This chapter's main study revolves around Greg, an extravert, and Emily, an introvert. Greg loves to have dinner guests on a Friday evening as a standing tradition but Emily is never comfortable on these evenings. While their relationship is generally good, these Friday evenings have been a source of conflict throughout their relationship. Emily dislikes them and dreads Friday evenings. Greg, on the other hand, enjoys the evenings and finds Emily's avoidance of them to be a sign that she is anti-social and that she really doesn't care about his feelings.

At the outset, Greg tends to be a lot louder and, as a result, Emily starts to withdraw. She does feel guilty about not wanting to attend the evenings and this causes her to feel defensive. Greg sees her withdrawal as a sign that she really doesn't care and the situation becomes more and more negative.

What Cain suggests in situations such as this is that both parties need to truly try and understand how their ingrained personalities influence how they communicate and what they need. Greg should understand that Emily prefers social settings to be more intimate so she is anti-social in these situations. He should also try to understand that her withdrawal during conflict or from social encounters is more about her personal preferences than a sign that she doesn't care.

Emily should understand that Greg believes that confrontation is healthy, even when it is uncomfortable. She could start to learn that direct communication can lead to a healthier relationship over the long term. She could acquire more communication skills so she can participate without feeling too uncomfortable.

In the end, the pair came to a suitable compromise. They halved the number of dinners and also changed the way in which the dinners were done so that both parties could enjoy them. They changed from a formal setting to a more informal buffet style that allowed guests to congregate in smaller groups. This allowed Emily to engage in more intimate interactions while still allowing Greg to interact with a lot of people.

Cain points out that working on an understanding of how someone with opposite traits interacts when it comes to social situations and what they need in terms of the quantity of interactions can help to make relationships run more smoothly.

CHAPTER 11
ON COBBLERS AND GENERALS

This chapter is about finding practical solutions for those who have children that are introverted. She leads off with a tale of a cautionary nature – of parents who are extroverted and have extroverted children. As the child differed so much from them, the parents enrolled the child in therapy to make them better. Their first attempts failed as the therapist was convinced that the child was not "damaged" but looked at things in a different way. The parents moved on until they found a therapist who agreed with them. The first therapist, however, was reluctant to assist in a situation where therapy may have done more harm than good.

Parents who suspect that their children are introverted need to find out how their children process their world and experiences and give a supportive, non-judgmental environment. Then they should indicate that that there is nothing wrong with this perception. Parents can encourage their children to attempt new experiences as long as there is no implied judgement. If you have an introverted child, try to understand that your child may need a higher feeling of safety before attempting something new.

If you want to add some variety into their daily lives, look for ways to help them to take small, less scary steps while at the same time reassuring them that their fear is only natural and you feel their feelings are important. It is also important to avoid overstimulating the child – progress in small steps so that your child is not overwhelmed.

Children that are exposed to this kind of coaching are able to learn how important being self-reliant is and this helps them cope as adults.

Cain gives more practical hints when it comes to the introvert and situations involving large groups of people like school. She encourages parents to get to school early and let their child become more acquainted with the place before the other kids arrive. It may be a good idea to introduce the child to their teacher before classes start. It can be helpful to teach the child to fake confidence so that they are better able to deal with difficult situations.

Cain now focuses on the environment at school. She makes suggestions that teachers and administrators can use to help understand and meet the needs of children that are introverted. Parents need to think about features that will make the school environment more conducive for learning for schooling their kids. Current research shows that introverts make up around a third to a half of our population. It is not something for which we need a cure but it is something we should make allowances for. Teachers need to look for ways in which kids who are introverted can express themselves and actively participate. When working in groups, it would be better to keep these smaller and to properly define the roles of the children within the group. It is useful for the extroverted students to learn to work on their own and to learn how to be more focused. Trying to force the interaction issue will seldom turn out well and could damage the confidence of the introverted kids. You can get around this by allowing them to make the decision of whether to work alone or in teams.

As a parent, you can help your child practice the strategies to help them succeed and also help them to find their personal sanctuary – at school and home. It is important to offer a non-judgmental sounding board for your child to express his/her feelings. If your child begins to believe that you feel that some reactions are incorrect, then they will soon stop sharing with you and you will miss out in communication. As a parent, you can be both supportive of your child's interests and help them bridge gaps in the social structures that they must deal with. It is important to remember that introverts have great strengths in creativity and understanding as these relate to what they are passionate about. To bolster their self-esteem, you need to support them in their endeavors.

CONCLUSION

To conclude this book, Cain runs through the basic takeaways of the book. She re-iterates that the extrovert ideal is not the only worthwhile ideal and that introverts need to value their own strengths rather than conforming to the societal norms. It is worthwhile to try to understand the various ways that people interact and communicate with one another and this is essential when supporting others.

By developing a better understanding of introverts and how they engage with the world and finding out what obstacles there are in a world where extroverts are thought of as something to strive for, you can learn how to help your introverted child succeed. Managers and teachers are able to derive benefits from understanding how introverts study and work so that they can be guaranteed to use the talents these people possess to best advantage.

ANALYSIS

Overall this was quite an ambitious project to tackle and covers a wealth of information. It is difficult not to be impressed by the in-depth coverage of introversion. Cain has dealt with each strata of society and worked through a great amount of research across various disciplines in order to back up her theories and build credibility. This book excels in the identification of the extrovert ideal as is currently popular in American culture. Cain offers well-reasoned arguments about the historic nature of this ideal and how it is too rigid in its definition of the ideal person, to the detriment of people who are introverted and their contributions. She deals harshly with the current view that the extrovert ideal is the best one to strive toward.

She doesn't just lay out the theory though – she backs it up with advice that can be applied by introverts to help them succeed. Her suggestions have been made with the introvert in mind and should be well received by them. Her personal experience at being made to conform gives her unique insight and allows her to offer tips to copy extroversion, when needed, and to optimize the unique skills that make introverts valuable. The one complaint is that the advice should have been the main focus of the book as that would be more interesting to most readers.

There is a lot of time spent on defining extroversion and introversion and this can become a little too much. Considering that this is a book for laypeople more than experts, it would have been enough to simply provide a basic definition and to state that psychological definitions can be contentious at best. She could have included further details in her footnotes for those interested. The amount of detail that Cain has included here is quite distracting for most readers.

Chapter 8 dealing with the differences between Eastern and Western culture is not her finest moment. Cain comes across as seeming to doubt her claims here. The author, though trying to avoid stereotypes, doesn't quite manage to do so. The simple truth of the matter is that defining a "national identity" as was done here is problematic because it fails to account for differences in personalities. Those who have studied culture or anthropology may find this chapter hard to swallow. The overall theme can also be questionable. The primary argument in this chapter is that the extrovert ideal is a cultural construct rather than a natural progression. This point, however, was alluded to in the opening chapter and so chapter 8 was unnecessary.

In a similar manner, parts of Chapter 6 are also disappointing. Neither Cain nor Aron, whose research she is drawing on, have any expertise when it comes to evolutionary biology. In addition, the stories that are oversimplified and couched in language that sounds sociobiological are acknowledged as one of the reasons why this discipline sometimes ranks badly amongst other disciplines. The chapter doesn't really add much to the overall conclusions in the book and could have been discarded. In addition, Cain seems to have focused on developmental psychology without exploring different perspectives from different disciplines of psychology. Had she explored these as well, she would have been better able to make the point that we can change our temperament.

Finally, the weakness of this book is that Cain spent so much time making the point that introverts should be valued that she has come across as anti-extrovert and belittling their contributions. It sometimes seems as though the author wants to stress that being introverted is the new ideal to strive for.

However, this book is worth spending time on, for both introverts and extroverts. Some of the criticism that has been leveled at this book is about how much it covers and how ambitious it is. Everyone stands to learn something when reading this book, whether about themselves or others. The primary arguments that the book presents are scientifically sound and the insights into the character of introverts as these relate to performance are likely to benefit managers, teachers, parents and partners.

CONNECT WITH ANT HIVE MEDIA!

THANK YOU FOR READING!

We hope you enjoyed this summary version of the book and took something away from it. Let us know what you learned and help others by leaving a review.

Want more?
Visit
www.anthivemedia.com/freesummaries
to receive your pack of (5) e-book summaries
FREE!

Check us out on Instagram:
www.instagram.com/anthivemedia/

Follow along on Facebook:
www.facebook.com/AntHiveMediaSocial

CPSIA information can be obtained
at www.ICGtesting.com
Printed in the USA
LVOW04s1036250416

485095LV00055B/913/P

9 781530 954070